D1297845

ADAPTED BY NANCY E. KRULIK
FROM THE SCREENPLAY WRITTEN BY
TOM S. PARKER & JIM JENNEWEIN

ISBN 0-590-25087-6

Richie Rich and all Characters ® & © Harvey Comics Inc.,
a Harvey Entertainment Company, 1994.
Copyright © Warner Bros., 1994
ALL RIGHTS RESERVED. Published by Scholastic Inc.

Book designed by N.L. Kipnis

12 11 10 9 8 7 6 5 4 3 2 1   4 5 6 7 8 9/9

Printed in the U.S.A   24

First Scholastic printing, December 1994

SCHOLASTIC INC.

New York   Toronto   London   Auckland   Sydney

As far as most of the kids in town were concerned, Richie Rich was one lucky boy!

He lived in a huge mansion. Famous baseball players taught him how to bat and field. Helicopters took him to and from important appointments, and amusement park rides went round and round right in his own backyard.

2

   As far as Richie Rich was concerned, the other kids in town were the real lucky ones.
   They had the one thing Richie wanted more than anything in the world — friends their own age! It could be pretty lonely being around grown-ups all the time.

Richie Rich was the son of Richard Rich Senior, the wealthiest man in the world. Mr. Rich was also one of the most beloved men in the world, because he used so much of his money to help other people.

Mr. Rich was a businessman. And he had a lot of fun with his businesses — especially with the crazy products he and his pal Professor Keenbean invented together!

4

Richie loved to go into the lab and watch Professor Keenbean work. The Professor was just a little wacky. His experiments were always amazing things, like his new stain remover — a chemical that not only removed spots, but made any fabric instantly dirtproof, waterproof, and bulletproof!

"This could be the biggest thing since your father and I invented the micro-chip and the ice-cream sandwich!" the professor said to Richie.

Richie grinned. Once again, his dad was part of something big!

5

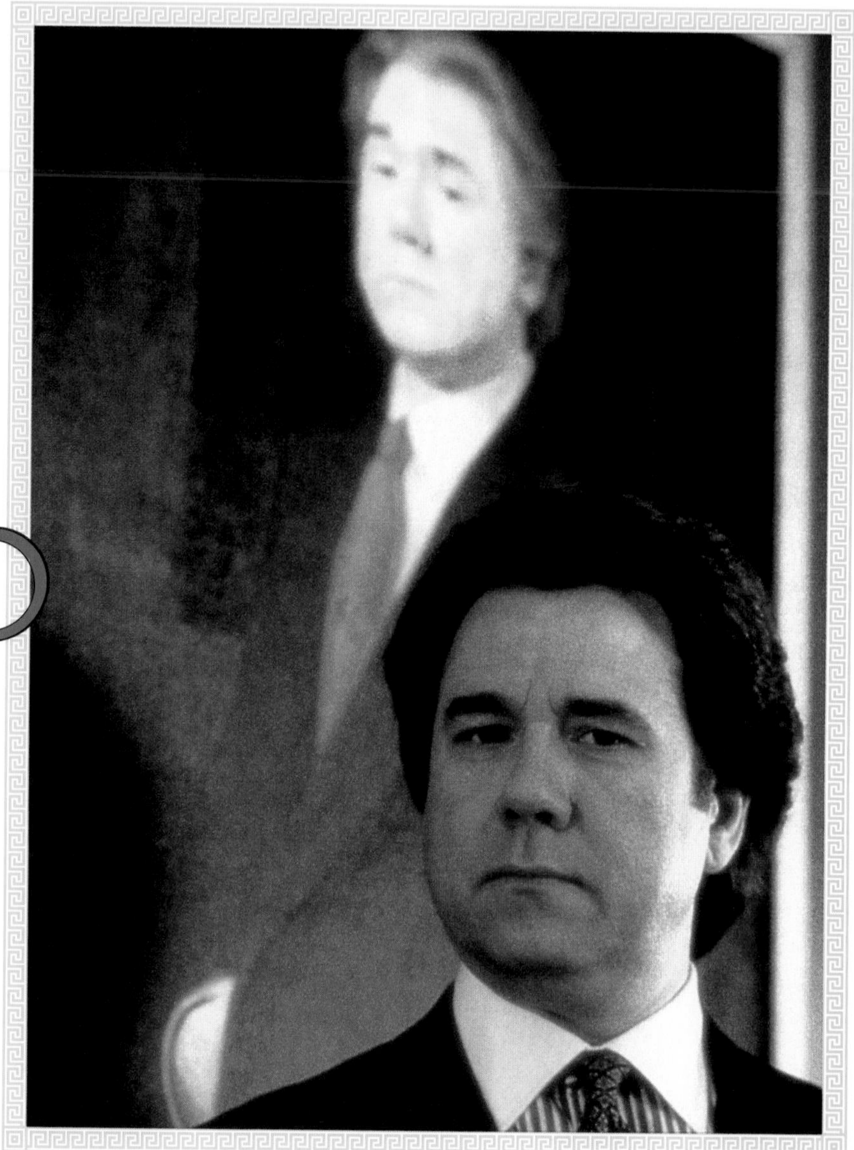

Richie hoped that someday he could grow up to be like his dad — smart, kind, and loved by everyone.

But of course, Mr. Rich was not really loved by everyone. One man hated him — a lot! That man was Laurence Van Dough, the son of Mr. Rich's former partner. Laurence Van Dough was so angry with Mr. Rich that he plotted with the Riches' bodyguard, Ferguson, to kill Mr. Rich, his wife Regina, and Richie! That way Van Dough could take over Rich Industries and all of the treasures in the family vault!

"Finally my father will have his revenge," Van Dough told Ferguson.

"Forty years ago my father founded this company."

Ferguson butted in. "Your father, sir? I thought Mr. Rich's father . . . "

"Well, yes, he started it, too," Van Dough harumphed. "But twenty-five years ago, they parted company. My father wanted to run the business like a business. Mr. Rich wanted to run it like a charity ward. My father died penniless and left me with nothing."

Ferguson looked at Van Dough with surprise. "I thought you had a trust fund. Ten million dollars."

Van Dough was furious. "Practically nothing!" he shouted. "But in a few short hours, I'll be Chairman and CEO of Rich Industries!"

Van Dough's dastardly plot went into action the very next morning when Mr. and Mrs. Rich and Richie were scheduled to fly their private airplane to London to meet with the Queen.

If Van Dough had his way, the Riches would never make it to supper at Buckingham Palace!

Everything started out exactly as Van Dough had planned. The Riches boarded their private jet, just as they always did. Mrs. Rich taxied down the runway, just as she always did. And when the plane took off it was time for lunch.

"Some sandwiches, darling?" Mr. Rich asked.

"That'd be great," his wife answered. "But don't go sneaking any of those chocolates. They're for the Queen."

Mr. Rich laughed and made his way to the back of the plane. There he spotted some wrapped packages — gifts for the Queen. Mr. Rich thought about those chocolates. Maybe if he snuck just one, no one would notice.

But which box held the treats?

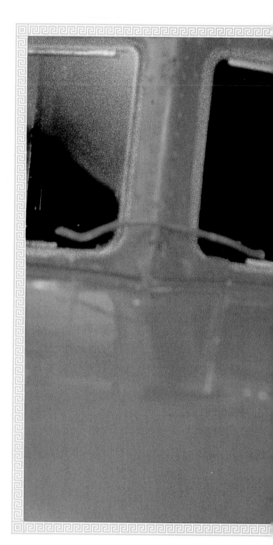

To find out, Mr. Rich grabbed one of the professor's newest inventions — the Smellmaster. One sniff and the machine could tell what was inside anything. He held the Smellmaster up to one parcel.

"Seventeen-grain pearls," it said mechanically.

Mr. Rich picked up a brightly wrapped red package.

"Trinitrotoluene," the Smellmaster reported.

Mr. Rich ran to the front of the plane. "Darling, there's no tag on this gift," he said. "The Smellmaster says it's trinitrotoluene. If I remember correctly that's the proper name for . . ."

"TNT!" they shouted together.

Swiftly, Mr. Rich opened the emergency door on the airplane and threw the package into the ocean below. The bomb exploded in a huge fireball, tearing off part of the plane's tail!

Back in the United States, Van Dough was celebrating his good fortune. He held up a glass and toasted himself. "To the new chairman of Rich Industries — me."

But Van Dough was wrong. It seemed Richie Rich, the sole heir to the Rich business and fortune, was not on the plane. At the last minute, he had decided to stay home. And while Van Dough was celebrating, Richie was doing something he had never done before. He was playing with kids his own age.

11

Richie's butler, Herbert Cadbury, knew that Richie would have no fun in England, where he would spend all his time with grown-ups. So Cadbury had asked permission for Richie to remain at home. Then Cadbury rounded up some children and brought them to Richie's mansion for a special day of fun. At first, the kids didn't want to visit. But once they saw the Rich mansion, they knew they'd come to the right place. The mansion was incredible — a huge, sprawling home with a giant mountain behind it. Carved into the mountain were the faces of Richie and his parents. They called it Mount Richmore.

"Whoa! It ain't no house, man," said Omar. "It's a whole 'hood!'"

"This place probably has its own zip code," Tony said.

The mansion may not have had its own zip code, but it did have quite a few other amazing features — like a whole fleet of motorbikes, a scary roller coaster that Richie got for Christmas, and best of all, a McDonald's!

"He's got his own Mickey D's" Omar exclaimed. "No way!"

Richie spent the whole day playing with his new friends. He was certain that this would be the best day of his whole life!

But then, Cadbury arrived to tell Richie that his parents' plane had been reported missing.

13

Richie stared in disbelief. This couldn't be happening to him! Richie ran right up to his room and tried to locate his dad, using his computer.

"Computer, locate Dad!" Richie commanded the machine.

The computer began its search for Mr. Rich. After what seemed like forever, the computer responded. "Dad not found," it said.

Richie was upset, but he still believed his parents had survived. "They are alive, Cadbury," he said bravely. "I know it!"

The following day, at nine o'clock sharp, Van Dough got to work undoing all of the wonderful things Mr. Rich had done. The first thing he did was close down the factory where the parents of Richie's new friends worked.

Richie's friend Gloria called Richie with the bad news. "It's your dad's company," she said to him. "Can't you do something?"

Richie certainly *could* do something, and he headed right down to his dad's office to do it!

Richie stormed out of his limousine and marched into his dad's office at Rich Industries. He was shocked to see Van Dough sitting at his dad's desk.

"Why are you in my father's office?" he asked.

"Because running the company can be done more efficiently from here," Van Dough answered.

Richie grinned. Van Dough wouldn't have to worry about that anymore.

"Until my parents come back," he said as he sat in his father's chair, "I've taken a sabbatical from school. So I can be here to run things. And by the way, the United Tool Company stays open!"

Richie began to follow in his father's footsteps. He worked out ways for the company to save money — without getting rid of anyone's jobs. He simply asked his father's chief executives to give up some of their money. That made Van Dough angry. But not as angry as he got a little later in the day . . . when he discovered that Richie had hired his friends to be his research team, and together they had increased business in Rich Candies. Richie was becoming a real success!

As far as Van Dough was concerned, Richie had to be stopped! He developed a cruel plan. The first thing he did was tell the police that Cadbury had murdered Mr. and Mrs. Rich. It wasn't true of course, but the police arrested him anyway.

With Cadbury in jail, there was no one to watch Richie. So, Van Dough went to court and had himself appointed Richie's guardian. That meant he could tell Richie what to do. It also put him in charge of Rich Industries, and of the Rich family's vault!

Next, Van Dough forced Richie to stay in the house. He posted guards at every entrance to make sure the boy did not escape. Then he set up an elaborate security system in an old closet. He even placed cameras at every entrance to the house.

Luckily, Richie had a good friend in the mansion — Professor Keenbean. Professor Keenbean also believed the Riches were still alive. And he was sure *Van Dough* had had Cadbury arrested. The professor helped Richie come up with a plan to rescue Cadbury. Soon Richie was sneaking out of the mansion on his way to the jail to help his pal Cadbury escape.

20

Cadbury felt happy to be out of the dirty jail cell — even if his new clothes weren't up to his usual neat style. Like Richie and Professor Keenbean, Cadbury believed that the Riches were alive. Perhaps together they could find Richie's parents, and stop Van Dough before he did much more damage!

Meanwhile, Van Dough had his own plans for Professor Keenbean. The professor was Mr. Rich's closest friend. Surely he knew where the Rich family vault was. Van Dough would force Keenbean to let him into the vault, and then the Riches' greatest treasures would be all his!

At first the good professor would have nothing to do with the evil plot.

"I told you I don't know where the vault is," Keenbean said.

Ferguson pulled tightly on the professor's necktie.

"And even if I did know where it was, it wouldn't do you any good," the professor gulped. "Because the lock is voice-activated. Only Mr. or Mrs. Rich can get in."

Van Dough was furious. Now how was he going to get into the vault? After all, Van Dough was certain that Mr. Rich was dead, and that he himself had killed him!

But, as usual, Van Dough was wrong. Mr. and Mrs. Rich were alive. They were floating along on a life raft. Mr. Rich had used the electrical parts from Mrs. Rich's razor and manicure tools to create a special signal machine that would beam a signal off a Rich Aerospace satellite and into Richie's computer. At that moment, Richie would be able to learn his parents exact position!

With Cadbury free, Richie was on his way to visit his friend Gloria. But that didn't mean Richie was giving up on finding his dad. He was just going to use Gloria's computer to do it. Cadbury and Diane watched nervously as Richie typed the words "Find Dad" into the computer. Then he typed in his own password, "SLUGGER."

Back in Richie's room, Richie's computer was tracing Mr. Rich. Richie hoped the computer would send the information to Gloria's machine. He was right! Suddenly the words "Dad found," flashed on the computer screen! Richie got excited! "They're alive!" he shouted. Now Richie knew the truth.

Unfortunately, Richie wasn't the only one who knew that his folks were alive! Ferguson had been in Richie's room back at the mansion. He saw the words on the computer screen, too. As soon as he did, he switched off the computer. Richie could get no more information from Gloria's computer.

"Mr. Van Dough," Ferguson called. "Good news, sir. Looks like we've found a way into that vault after all!"

25

Richie tried and tried to get Gloria's computer to work. But he could not. There was only one thing to do — Richie would have to sneak back into his house and use his own computer. It took a lot of doing, but with the help of Cadbury and his new friends, Richie made it safe and sound back to his room. He hooked up his computer and tried to locate his parents. That's when the strangest thing happened.

"I got it, Cadbury," he said to his trusted servant. "I got their location. Wait . . . his can't be right, it says Mom and Dad are here. Right inside the house!"

26

But Richie's computer was right. Ferguson and Van Dough had beaten Richie to his computer, found his parents, and brought them back to the mansion. It was part of Van Dough's plan. He would force Mr. Rich to open the vault. Then Van Dough would make off with the Riches' most valued treasures!

"The vault, Richard," Van Dough said with an evil laugh. "You show me the vault and no one will get hurt."

Mr. Rich shook his head sadly. He had no choice but to cooperate. Slowly he led Van Dough to Mount Richmore.

"Your vault's a whole mountain?" Van Dough asked with amazement. "You must be filthy rich!"

Van Dough stood at the vault door and held his breath. In a few seconds, the Rich family's valuables would be his. He closed his eyes and imagined the diamonds, rubies, and emeralds that would be there as the door slid open. But when he opened his eyes he saw . . . baby pictures, baseball cards, and bowling trophies!

"What is this?" Van Dough demanded. "Where's the gold, the diamonds, the money? Where is the money?"

"In banks," Mrs. Rich said.

Now Van Dough was really angry. He ordered one of his men to shoot the Riches.

"What's the matter, Mr. Van Dough?" Richie called from the vault doorway. "You don't have the guts to shoot anyone, do you Mr. Van Dough?"

Van Dough did have the guts. He aimed his gun and shot it at Richie. But Richie kept walking towards him. The bullets bounced right off of him. Professor Keenbean was right — the new stain remover did make things bulletproof!

Mr. Rich pounced on Van Dough. With a crash, piles and piles of bowling trophies fell from a shelf. Van Dough was buried in junk!

As Van Dough struggled to free himself, Richie's friends ran to get the police and the Riches raced out of the vault. "I know another way out," Mr. Rich shouted. His family followed him.

Unfortunately, Van Dough did, too.

The Riches raced through a passageway high up on a mountain. "Oh my goodness," Mrs. Rich cried out when she saw where she was standing. The Rich family was climbing Mount Richmore!

Ferguson was hot on their trail. He spotted a laser gun on a ledge. The laser was being used to put the finishing touches on the faces of Mount Richmore. Ferguson tried to use it to finish off the real Riches. He fired a shot at the path beneath the family. The family raced around the mountain trying to avoid the blasts from the laser gun. Ferguson was getting closer and closer.

But Ferguson had forgotten that Cadbury was still walking around free. All at once, the faithful servant appeared, and punched Ferguson in the jaw. The laser gun popped out of his hand.

Van Dough was watching the action from below. Now was his chance. He climbed up on the bridge of Mr. Rich's stone glasses and aimed his gun at Mr. Rich. But Cadbury was too fast for him.

He grabbed the laser gun, pointed it at the giant glasses, and fired. The rock shattered, Van Dough lost his grip and slipped down onto the sculpture's nose.

"Hey Dad," Richie laughed, "I know how you feel about firing people, but . . . "

"Well, Richie, in this case I think we can make an exception. Why don't you do the honors."

Richie looked down at Van Dough. He was swinging like a bug on Mr. Rich's nose. "Mr. Van Dough, you're fired!" he said.

With Van Dough and Ferguson in jail, the Rich family could finally relax. Richie was happy to have his parents home. To celebrate, he invited all of his new friends back to the mansion for a great game of baseball. His parents were there to cheer him on.

"Now our son is the richest boy in the world," Mr. Rich said to his wife as they watched him play with his pals.

Richie smiled at his folks. He couldn't have agreed more!